People Who Breathe

A Standing Qigong Sequence

Gene Smithson

 803 Lambeth Lane

Austin Texas 78748

waldosmithson@yahoo.com

Cover and interior design by: Gene Smithson

ISBN: 9798640751260   First Edition

Disclaimer: Information in this book is distributed "As Is," without warranty. Nothing in this document constitutes a legal opinion nor should any of its contents be treated as such. Neither the authors nor the publisher shall have any liability with respect to information contained herein. Further, neither the authors nor the publisher have any control over or assume any responsibility for websites or external resources referenced in this book. When it comes to martial arts, self-defense, violence, and related topics, no text, no matter how well written, can substitute for professional, hands-on instruction. The information contained in this manuscript is not to be taken as medical advice or a substitution for medical advice. Please consult with your Dr before beginning any exercise program. These materials should be used for academic study only.

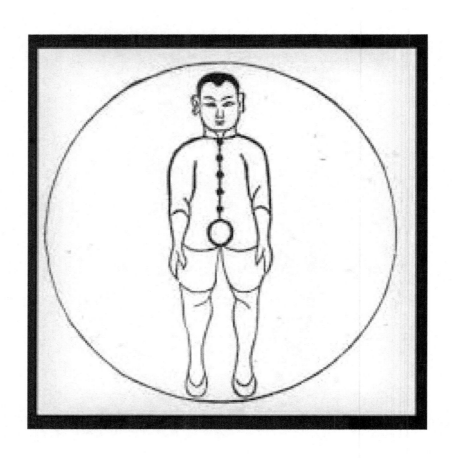

呼吸人
Hūxī rén

People of the Breath

Originally was: 空   Kong

人   Ren

People who breathe in nature. Natural people. People who know stillness. Movement within, stillness without.

Table of contents

Introduction

Qigong is an ancient Chinese practice dating as far back as 6000 years. Roughly translated it means to craft energy. More usefully it means to gather, cultivate, refine and manifest energy.

There are martial qigong practices, medical qigong practices and spiritual, or alchemical qigong practices, and of course, most blur the lines between all three, at least a little.

I am not a Master of qigong. I have trained in martial art for over 40 years and in these practices for over 20 years and am barely a beginner. I have, however; had the luxury and privilege of learning from two Masters of qigong.

Teng, YingBo is an extraordinary man I met on a cool morning in Beijing, China. He is a true Master of qigong in every sense of the word. He is still out there, practicing his magic, performing feats the defy belief. I cannot tell you how to find him, he found me.

Jesse Lee Parker has studied Taoist internal arts for his entire life. He has learned from and trained under, the greatest Masters of Taoist arts in the world having spent years in China in deep study, in remote areas. Sifu Parker currently resides in Japan and teaches and shares his vast knowledge with students all over the globe.

All credit for this sequence goes to Professor Teng, YingBo and Jesse Lee Parker, any criticism should be pointed right at me, the author.

This small pamphlet barely scratches the surface of the practice of qigong, however; Qigong need not be a complicated endeavor. Sometimes, the simplest practices explore and produce the deepest transformations.

With Love for all who enter into practice,

gene

Notes on the practice of qigong:

Wear loose and comfortable clothing.

If possible, the clothing should be of natural fiber rather than synthetic.

Practice outdoors when possible

If you practice indoors always crack a window or door

Optimal times for practice are dawn, sunset, noon and midnight

Best to practice on empty stomach

Study as much as you wish, but nothing takes the place of actual practice

Ignore the advice of the master's at your peril

Seek out a good teacher, we all need them

Training under the supervision and guidance of a teacher is safer and more productive

Qigong practice can be dangerous and may exacerbate mental instability, seriously

FIND A GOOD TEACHER

Train with a good and True heart

Pay much attention to Nature

Wuji

Beginning Posture

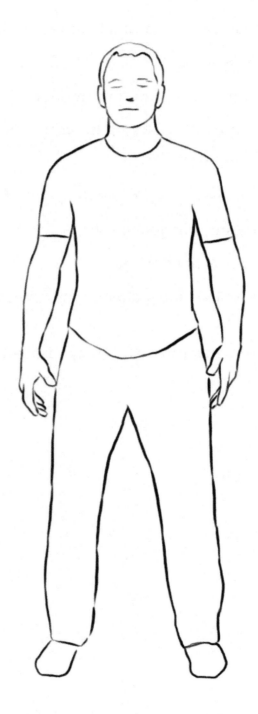

- Place the feet shoulder width apart.

- Lift the toes and create an arch in the foot; then relax toes down to floor.

- Soften the knees, let the kneecap fall.

- Lift the crown of the head (baihui).

- Relax the lower back and loosen the hips.

- Feel long space between lower ribs and hip points.

- Relax the eyes, the tongue, the face and the scalp.

- Relax the neck and balance the head atop the cervical spine.

- Relax trapezius and shoulders, upper arms and elbows; relax the forearms, wrists and hands.

- Relax the chest and the upper back.

- Relax the upper abdomen and the middle back.

- Relax the lower back and the lower abdomen.

- Relax hips, gluteal muscles, abductor and adductor muscles. Instability will come to the posture; this is good. Relax more deeply.

- Relax thighs and knees.

- Relax lower leg, gastrocnemius and soleus muscles.

- Relax ankles and feet.

- Posture will be unstable; every heartbeat and every breath will cause movement. Allow instability.

- Work to stack bones so that skeleton is standing without muscular tension.

- Open armpits enough so that air can touch skin in armpit.

- Lift crown. Remain still. Exhaling relax more and more deeply.

- This is okay to stand for an hour or more.

- Smile.

WARNING

Do not lock knees. You will pass out and fall on your face or worse.

Taiji

Balanced Between Heaven and Earth is Human

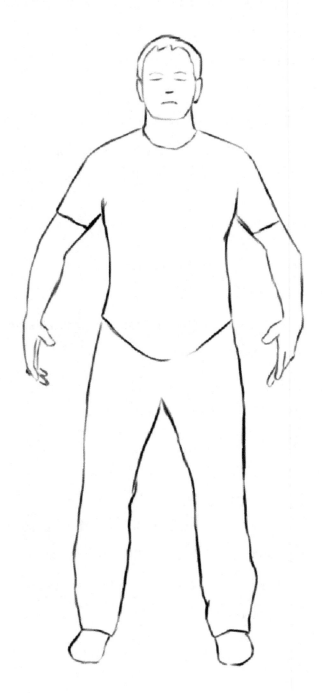

Inhale Yang from the Heavens and Yin from the Earth

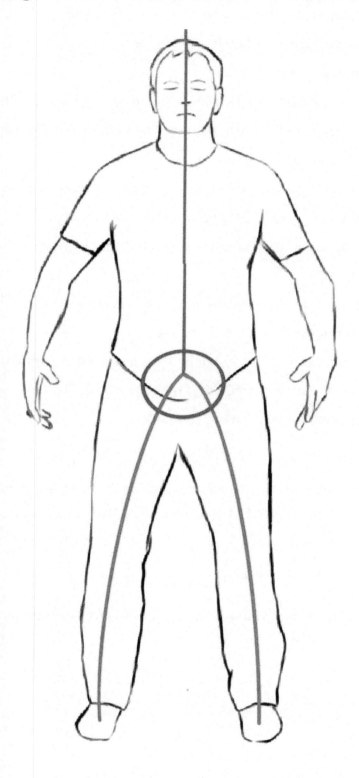

- Lift the crown and sink the shoulders.
- Create space in armpits, as if a grape were held there and would not fall or be crushed.
- Palms face sides of thighs (IT band).
- Knees are soft, not locked.
- Inhale Yang energy from the Heavens through the crown (baihui), down through the center of the body, into the lower dantien (just below the belly button and in).
- Repeat for 3, 9, 36 or 108 times.
- Inhale Yin energy from the Earth up through the soles of your feet (yong quan or bubbling wells), up through both legs into the lower dantien.
- Repeat for 3, 9, 36 or 108 times, it is suggested that you match the number of Yin and Yang pulling breaths
- Breathe Yang energy from the Heavens down through the crown and Yin energy from the Earth up through the feet simultaneously
- Allow the two energies to mingle, stir and mix in the lower dantien.
- Balanced between Heaven and Earth is the True Human Being.
- Exhale and relax more deeply, more completely.

Visualization: Standing at the very peak of a mountain, waist deep in snow, grounded by the enormous rock, surrounded by the wide, blue sky.

WARNING

Do not lock knees. You will pass out and fall on your face or worse.

Cleansing

Drive Stale or Stagnant Qi Out of Body, Down into Earth

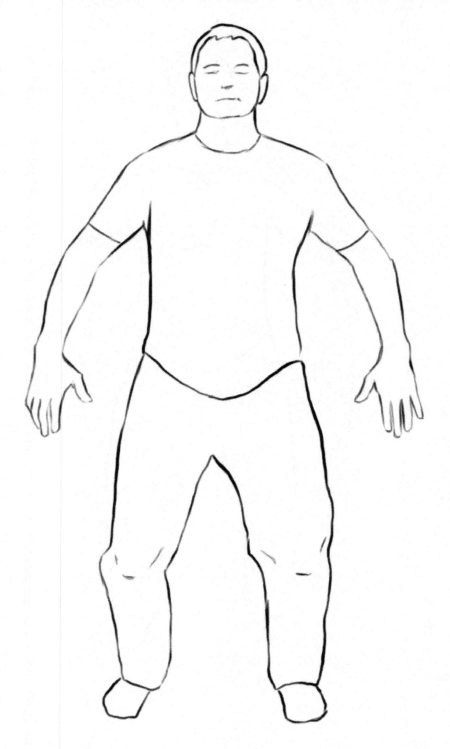

Drive Stale or Stagnant Qi Out of Body, Down into Earth

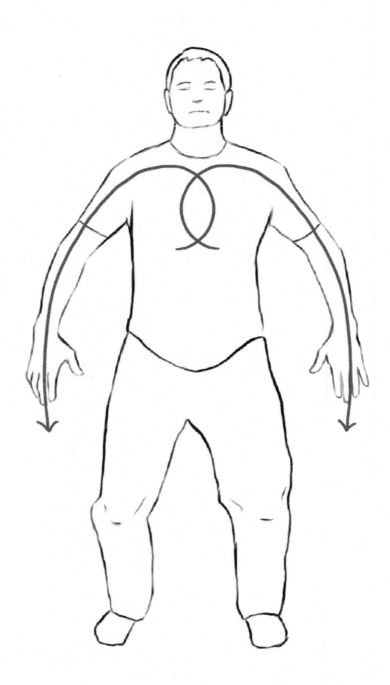

- Sink down. Bend the knees until you experience a tension spike in the thighs.
- Maintain tension in thighs for duration of posture.
- Rotate shoulders and forearms until palms face behind you.
- Press arms back until the palms are in the same plane as your back.
- Lift the crown and sink the shoulders.
- Keep space in armpit.
- Keep ears over shoulders, shoulders over hips and hips over ankles.
- Inhale and collect all the stale and stagnant qi within your body.
- Exhale and drive all stale and stagnant energy down the arms, out the fingers, down into the Earth.
- Earth transforms all, producing nurturing qi.

Visualization: Draw the brown and sticky thick qi from all the cells of your body as you inhale. Exhale, and the stale qi is driven down the arms and drips or streams off the ends of the fingers. Tension is kept in the thighs to block any immediate return. Earth will transform this gunk into beautiful, pure nurturing energy.

Extra instruction: This is very much a working posture. Intense mental effort and focus is required. Oft times the practitioner will sweat profusely.

WARNING

Keep tension in thighs. Can turn toes slightly inwards as extra precaution but not necessary.

Exchange Essence Qi

Skin as the Third Lung

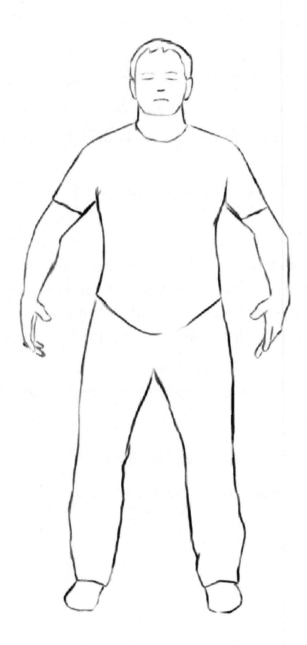

Skin as the Third Lung

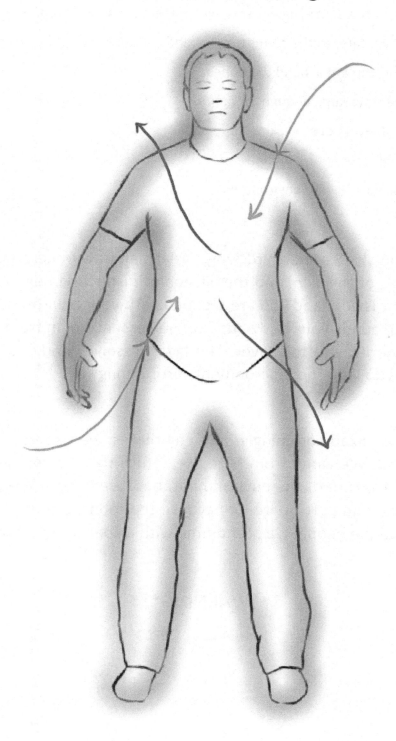

- Straighten legs until tension level drops.
- DO NOT LOCK KNEES. Keep knees soft, with kneecap (patella) dropped and loose.
- Allow arms to rotate, so the palms face IT bands or sides of thighs.
- Keep roundness in arms; bend the bones.
- Armpit space stays large enough for grape.
- Inhale through every pore in skin.
- Exhale through every pore in skin.
- Exchange Essence Qi with environment.

Visualization: The skin as the third lung. Breath and awareness flow in and out through the pores of the skin, and the illusion of distinction begins to evaporate. Your environment is you, and you are blended with your environment. It is as if a thermal layer surrounds your body and you pull essence qi in from this layer and exhale essence qi out into this layer. The layer dissolves and you truly begin to feel mixed in and up with the environment surrounding you.

Extra instruction: Mixed and mingled with all that is, we understand how we do not begin nor end. We came from here, we return to here, we never really left here at all. We take care of the environment, because it is us. We are mindful of what we consume and participate in, because the foods, the entertainment, the air and music, and the people we spend time with all become part of who we are.

WARNING

DO NOT LOCK KNEES

Ming-Men

Gate of Vitality (Life)

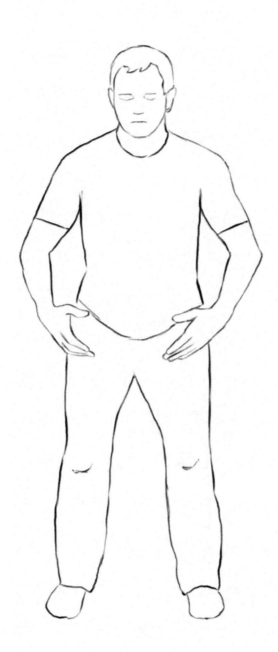

Ming-Men 1

Gate of Vitality

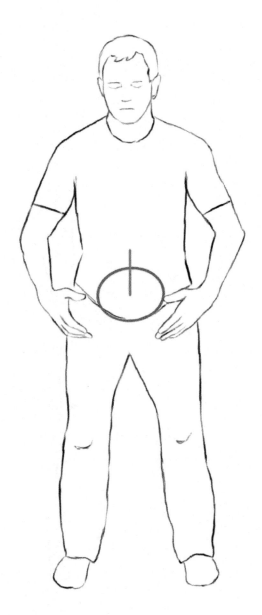

Ming-Men 2

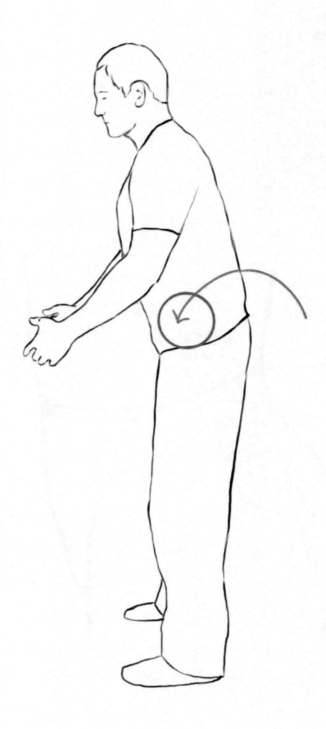

Ming-Men

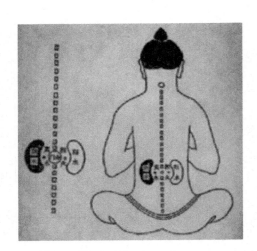

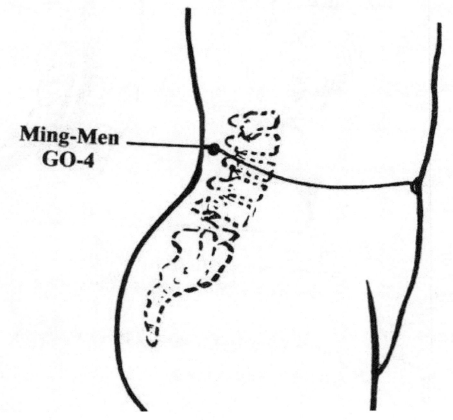

Ming-Men GO-4

- Allow the arms to move in front of the lower abdomen.

- Palms face lower dantien.

- Maintain space in armpits.

- Keep crown and spine aligned, but tip forward at the hip joints (femur heads).

- Torso is no longer perpendicular to Earth but is at a slight angle.

- Keep lower back free of tension. Do not bend over at waist. Fold at hips.

- Elongate the cervical spine: pull the crown to lengthen the spine.

- Arms are rounded; bend the bones.

- Inhale Yin energy through the Ming-Men.

- Draw the Yin energy through L4-L5 and into the lower dantien.

Visualization: Standing waist deep in a gently flowing stream, rest a beach ball on the surface of the water. Hold ball lightly but securely. Feel the stream sweeping gently along over the lower body. Feel the buoyancy of the large ball resting and pressing slightly down into the water.

Extra instruction: Exhale and relax. Don't rush this posture.

Zhan Zhaung

Stand Like a Tree

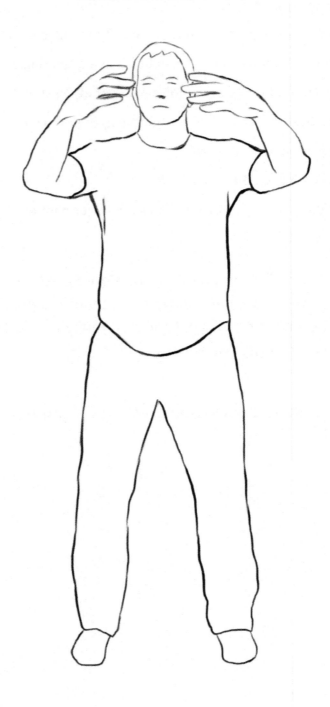

Standing Like a Post

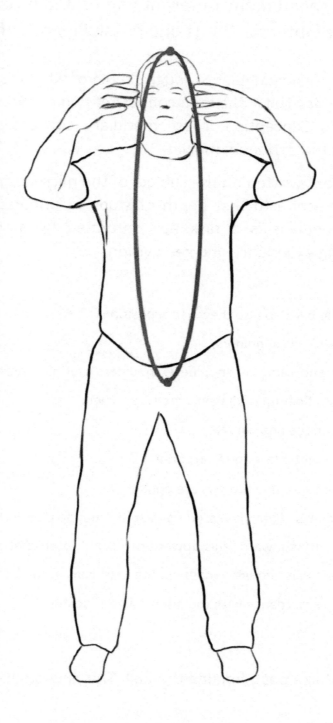

*** NOTE***

This posture is called many different names and is practiced with a variety of intents. This is one possibility out of many.

Further notes: This drawing depicts a rough sketch of what is sometimes referred to as the "microcosmic orbit." The loop consists of two meridians: the Du and the Ren, or Control and Conception. These meridians connect at the tongue and upper palate and at the perineum (huiyin).

There are entire books written on the subject of the microcosmic orbit. This small pamphlet does not aspire to that depth of study or understanding. Circulating energy through meridians is a task best informed by a teacher in physical proximity and of long experience and keen vision.

- Allow torso to tip back up into the vertical position.
- Lift the crown, sink the shoulders.
- Maintain alignment: ears over shoulders, shoulders over hips, hips over ankles.
- Allow the arms to float up until palms are throat high.
- Arms remain rounded and curved.
- Palms (laogong points) face the heart area.
- The knees remain soft, and armpits are open.
- The tongue remains slightly pressed against the upper palate, the perineum remains pulled upward, lifting inward. This upward pull is not intense at all. Very slight tension, almost intent alone, is enough to connect the meridians at the bottom juncture.
- Inhale, exhale in accordance with the intent of your posture.

Visualization: Stand like post, holding the ball. This is enough. Let the posture do the work.

WARNING

This posture is one of the most practiced and recognizable postures in all of internal martial art. Different traditions ascribe many different functions and purposes, and they are probably ALL CORRECT. When I began my practice of qigong in a serious way, my teacher cautioned me about too much study of written materials. He encouraged me to practice, just practice... and then MORE practice, so that when I encountered literature and terminology, I would have a solid grounding in my own experience first.

Too many people get trapped into chasing experiences that do not belong to them. They attempt to fulfill someone else's experience or expectation and become lost, absolute experts in verbiage, argument and advice, and bereft of any real experience or understanding of their own.

This is a sad, sad condition, one of great intellectual knowledge and no actual benefit. It is far better to approach the great mystery in awe and innocence, allowing the Universe to inform you, rather than you to define it.

Extra Instruction: Research microcosmic orbit, read entire books and attend seminars and clinics designed to study the phenomenon but...

Do your own work. Stand like a post and breathe and wait quietly. The truth will find you through actual practice.

Yang from the Heavens

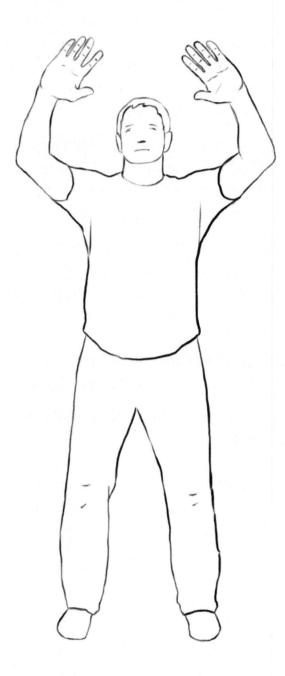

Yang Energy from the Heavens

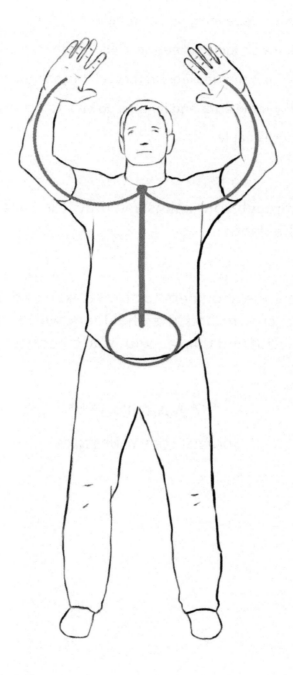

- Allow the forearms to rotate and rise slightly as the palms rotate to face away and out.
- Palms (laogong) face away from you and up towards the sky.
- Gaze is slightly upwards as if looking away and above the horizon. Eyes may be partially closed or lightly closed depending on environment.
- Lift the crown, sink the shoulders, keep space between the cervical vertebrae.
- Inhale Yang energy from the Heavens, in through the palms (laogong).
- Draw the energy down the arms and in, then down into the lower dantien.
- Exhale and relax more deeply.

Visualization: Inhale through your palms and draw the Yang energy down into the torso and down into the dantien.

Extra instruction: Allow the shoulders to stay relaxed and down. Don't pull them down. Rather, lift the crown, and the shoulders will drop naturally. Keep the lower back vertebrae loose and relaxed with space between.

WARNING

DO NOT LOCK YOUR KNEES

Yin from the Earth

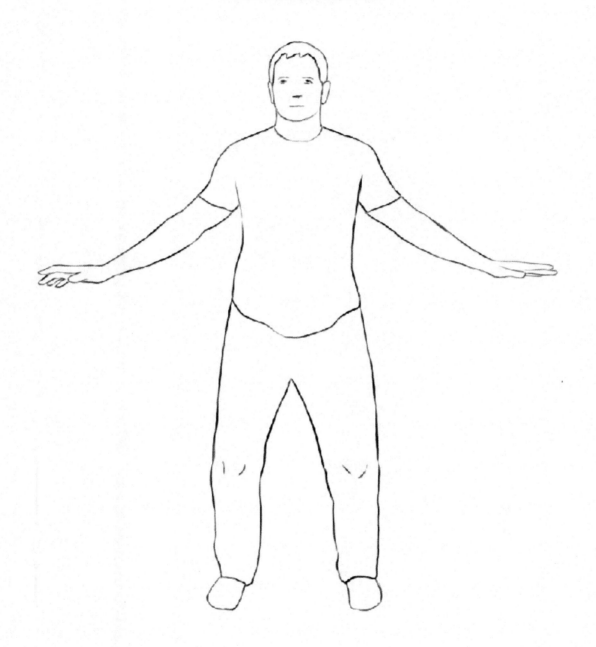

Yin Energy from the Earth

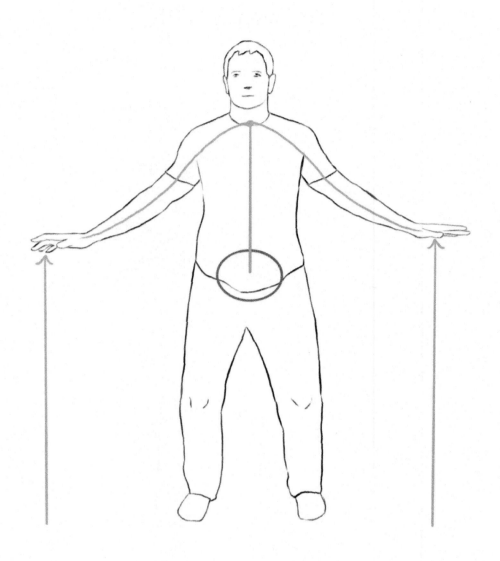

- Allow the arms to arc up and over as if to flap wings down.

- Press the palms (laogong) down until it is as if they are resting on two tabletops.

- Palms are facing the Earth.

- Keep space in the joints, arms, spine and legs. Bones are rounded and curved. Thighs are externally rotated, spiraling out and down.

- Sink down until tension spikes in the thighs.

- Lift the crown; sink the shoulders.

- Keep alignment: ears over shoulders, shoulders over hips, hips over ankles.

- Inhale Yin energy from the Earth, up through the palms (laogong).

- Draw the Yin energy up the arms and in, then down into lower dantien.

- Exhale and relax more deeply.

Visualization: Kindness as a loving Mother for a child flows up from the ground and into your palms. Draw the very feeling of nurture up your arms and in, then down gently and deeply into the lower dantien.

Extra instruction: SOFTEN. Gently, gently...relaxed and still mind. Open, trusting and loving heart.

WARNING

For many people, opening the joints in the arms produces a fair amount of burning pain, especially in the forearm, hand and elbow regions. With continued practice the connective tissues will release and relax and the burning feeling there will subside.

Wuji

Return

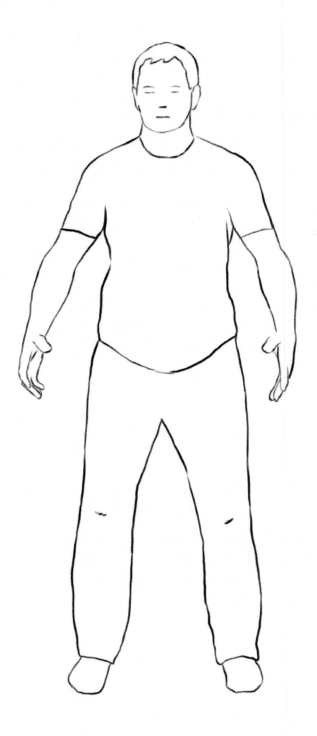

Return to Undifferentiated

Wuji and Return

Superimposed, one layered on top of the other, expansion from beginning of practice, to end.

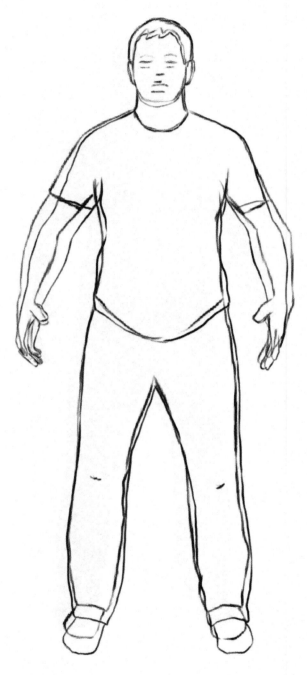

The return to Wuji. The cessation of duality.

- Allow the body to return to original posture.

- Lift the crown; sink the shoulders.

- Let the pelvic girdle dangle from a loose and relaxed space between the lumbar vertebrae.

- Knees are soft, patella dropped.

- Femurs spiral out and down.

- Feet are parallel and soft. Feel the connection between the Earth and the feet.

- Feel the size of your footprints expand, and you are grounded, rooted deeply in kindness and the seemingly inexhaustible compassion of Earth.

- Pulled between Heaven and Earth; balanced, suspended like a marionette.

- Spacious inside as the Universe.

- Inhale into your center, and allow the breath, your awareness to fill your torso and limbs, travelling out, expanding from your center to your extremities and crown.

- The inhale is thin and soft and long and quiet and gentle, continual.

- It is possible to expand even beyond the supposed boundary of the skin, growing out and expanding to include… to encompass…to hold within.

- Exhale and return to the body, the torso, the dantien and continue the exhale until…you have become infinitesimally small.

- And as the exhale fades into nothingness, as that quiet pause comes, you exist as undifferentiated, a part and the whole of the Universe at once, all the galaxies, and all the space.

- It is quiet. It is beautiful. There is a sound and an experience.

- Rest.

Depart the Mountain

Now that you have finished your standing practice for the moment you may find the following actions helpful.

- Slowly open eyes, blink carefully

- Place palms one atop the other on abdomen

- Massage gently in circles (9 counterclockwise and 9 clockwise)

- Rub arms down the outside and up the inside 3 times

- Rub legs down the outside and up the inside 3 times

- Fold hands closed with thumb inside covering laogong

- Vigorously scrub kidney area

- Massage face

- Massage scalp and ears

- Massage neck

This concludes the standing sequence instruction.

Terminology

Du mai or Du meridian (Governing or Control)

Ren mai or Ren meridian (Conception)

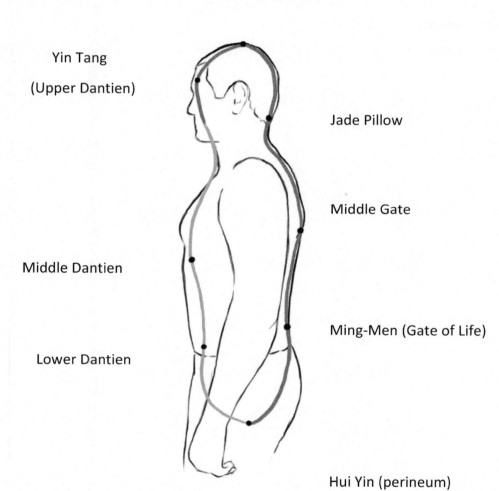

Bai Hui (crown)

Yin Tang

(Upper Dantien)

Jade Pillow

Middle Gate

Middle Dantien

Ming-Men (Gate of Life)

Lower Dantien

Hui Yin (perineum)

Acknowledgements:

Professor Teng, YingBo is a simply put, a master of qigong. He lives somewhere in China. With a little research you can probably find him. I was extremely fortunate that he found me. On a crisp October morning in Beijing this small man walked into my world and radically changed my life for the better. If you want to see movie magic type qigong, find Teng, YingBo and train with him.

Jesse Lee Parker is a master in his own right and has dedicated his entire life to the study of Taoist arts. Sifu Parker is currently available to teach various forms of qigong, taijiquan and internal alchemical practices.

These two men introduced me to qigong practice. Without their instruction, supervision, love and encouragement I would have been utterly lost; to these two men belong all the credit. Any criticism should be pointed right at me.

Disclaimers:

Any mistakes in this booklet belong solely to me. I have intentionally kept this a very simple introductory instruction. I initially put this pamphlet together for my students and not for outside consumption. I am releasing it to the public now, but with a plea and an admonishment.

Internal arts should be practiced under the supervision of an experienced practitioner or a master of the internal arts.

How will you know when you have found a genuine master of the internal arts? Now there is a great question.

When you are in the presence of a master of these arts, there is a palpable energy surrounding them. I describe it most simply as, feeling less vulgar in every sense.

These Internal Arts should not be approached lightly, as the energies unleashed by these simple postures can cause great harm. Key to safety and progress is Humility.

Closing thoughts:

I am no master of qigong. I put this pamphlet together to help my students with their home practice. I like the simplicity of the practice as it is presented here but be advised that it is incomplete. You, me... we need teachers to guide us and correct our missteps so...

Enjoy this pamphlet and use it as a very basic reference but find a True Master and train with their guidance.

Love,

gene

Printed in Great Britain
by Amazon

37296748R00024